M000215497

What's my Address?

by Lisa Ganser

A POOR Press / Prensa POBRE Publication

a POOR Press Publication ©2021

ISBN 978-1-956534-03-0

POOR Press is a poor and indigenous people-led press
dedicated to publishing the books and scholarship of youth,
adults, and elders in poverty locally and globally.

thank you to nomy lamm for design and copy editing
www.nomyteaches.com

www.poormagazine.org
www.poorpress.net

dedication

a gift for my brother and friend, Marty
so you know that you are loved
and that you exist

from current me
to older me
to remember

table of contents

1   long lines

3   tiny shithole apartments

5   an ocean of soda pop

7   my brother was born

12   call me if it gets bad

16   walk down to kmart to buy some shoes

17   jerry's leftovers

21   my mom's voice

23   trying to be cool

25   storage wars

29   survivor love letter

31   thank you auntie kare kare

tan britannias 34

i loved my mom like this 35

i can tell 37

a pantry, tv trays,
and a pillowcase full of loot 38

still housed haikus 41

no need for 911 42

bad babysitters 44

tomboy 48

weekends with dad 49

alone together 53

escape to the blueberries 55

acknowledgements 57

long lines

i come from long lines, norway, austria, ireland
of people who came,
escaping violence and poverty
and who Took.

sacrificing so that i
could even write a book
cutting across lands
through neighborhoods
like a sharp
familiar knife
in search of safety and opportunity
and a better white life

i am living to UNlearn the entitlement of "mine"
while having been evicted at least a dozen times

i used to think i couldn't keep one house plant alive
if i had a house for a plant, and even if i really tried
and that i'd die by suicide.

at 52 years old i am surrounded by living, loving,
plant medicine guides
going back to them
from where i came
in line behind Mothers, Femmes, Ancestors, Earth
there for me, like they have been
since even before my Birth

my fair, weathered

hands
are in dark, wet, wormy,
well tended soil.

a blueberry that i grew
explodes in my mouth.

i smell cedar so strong, under branches
like long arms, swooping so far down
they kiss the ground, some even taking root!
raising back up again to the sky

i think about my ancestor Momma, Sam
her strength, her wisdom, her trauma
her laugh lines, my punch lines, our blood lines
production lines, dead lines, life lines, front lines
factory lines, worry lines, welfare lines
queer lineage, transcestors, disabled ancestors
My Brother.

tending this patch of "rent to own" land
is now my Life's Work
in this one level, accessible,
just maybe "forever home"
on this Squaxin, Turtle Island Earth

tiny shithole apartments

i used to be there, i used to have that
that place, those things, familiar surroundings of Home
i can close my eyes to see it, even though the building
is literally demolished

the living alone, the guest rooms, studios, the cubicle

my name finally came up on the section 8 wait list,
and they couldn't track me down to let me know

uproot to a new place, leaning into medicines that bring chaos
i thought maybe the navy would help,
but they kicked me out too
cut across state lines, into a dry county
trying to pull my shit together
only to hear them say
"yer not even on the lease"
"there's not even one bill in your name"

Lost
so many things
in "storage"
Again

cell phone (brand new invention) rings
and after two plus years
of wait list, I am up to bat
for MICD (mental illness, chemically dependent)
dual diagnosis "supportive housing"

and uh-oh, couch surfing isn't considered "homeless"
so my current sitch is a swing and a miss

"have you stayed in a shelter in the past 6 months?"

i had to be UNhoused on paper
to access this "more permanent"
based on my income affordable Home

"could you go stay in a shelter tonite?"
but i already have a temporary roof
"oh! wait. you slept in a broken down bus
in someone's back yard
at some point this year!?!"
YES! and YAY
that qualifies.

if i live by myself, there's less people
to be hurt by me, to kick me out, break up
find someone better, discover that i am too much, neglect me
not pay the rent with the money i hand off
hand me money that i don't pay
tell me i'm in bed too much, not renew my lease

there was comfort in living just me and cat, dog, dogs
less ways to overstay a welcome, in my own
glorious
tiny shit hole apartments

when i am alone there is no fear
that the Trusted One is plotting to leave
or cut me loose, i mean the one i Trust
if i even Trust myself

4

an ocean of soda pop

we had a curfew, but we were free
playing soccer in the fresh cut grass
between the apartment buildings
until way past dark

we "borrowed" lumber from construction sites
and collectively built a tree fort
in one of the big trees in the woods behind the buildings
we were thirsty, so we went to grab something to drink

i was the oldest, big little instigator

we formed a line around the quick mart at the gas station
i was at the front of this little kid production line
tossing back 12 packs of soda
bam bam bam sending the sodas to the next set of hands
someone said, "slow down, there's too many to carry"
i threw more
pepsi, mountain dew, orange crush, mug root beer
we were living up to the marketing
and "having a pepsi day"

we struggled into the little wooded area behind the quick mart
having to stop and rest often
i was carrying six 12 packs myself, two in each hand
spreading my fingers to a painful point
and one under each arm
it was about a half mile walk on University Avenue
parading this huge load of pop so publicly
back to the apartment complex

we were almost to the tree fort when it started to rain
the downpour made our task harder, and we pushed on

there was enough soda to line two whole walls of the tree fort
solid!

we were cracking our first celebratory soda
didn't even get a sip
when we heard our Mom yell
"Lisa! Marty!" and she sounded angry
we knew to get our asses home
shit! how does she know?!?

we were scolded before we even opened the door
"do you know why i'm so mad?" our Mom asked

i'm so glad i didn't have time to answer

"your Dad is in town, he's been calling, he wants to pick you
kids up for the weekend. what are you thinking being out in
the rain?!?! yer drenched! you could get sick! get into some dry
clothes, pull together an overnight bag, your Dad will be here
any minute," she said.

i was relieved,
and triumphant!

on sunday when we came back, we were so excited to drink
our sodas and went right to the tree fort. as we got closer i
could see an ocean of empty soda cans on the ground. empty
cans filled the floor of the tree fort.

every can of soda had been swallowed up by the older kids.

what a load of crap. all we could do was clean up the mess.

my brother was born

i learned the beginnings
of how to be a People Protector
by being three
and having a younger Brother
Be Born

we were raised together
played together
for the first ten years of his life
with our Mom
bunk beds
played with cars
building out cityscapes in
the dry sand lot
of the apartment's front "yard"
a whole city!

having sword fights
with the cardboard from inside
the big wrapping paper rolls
at xmas
slappin' each other silly with 'em
til the cardboard swords
turned into flappy flailing cords
jumping on beds
laughing so hard
our Mom let us do it
that shit was the best

playing kick the can

hide and seek
soccer
football
after dark
with all the different neighborhood kids
in all the different neighborhoods
we had so much Freedom
an entire adventurous existence
outside of whatever place was Home
in parks, in the woods
in the sun
in the snow
under stars
just be within earshot
and GET HOME
when and if our Mother yells our names
"Marty!!! Lisa!!!"

he liked the tv on
kinda loud
in the other room at night
if no grown ups were around
i would leave the door ajar
so he could sleep
i kept creeps away from him
so he could stay asleep

he did not like mayonnaise
or anything that resembled mayonnaise
he did not like any of the foods
touching each other
when they were
on his plate.
i had to be the bad guy
to make sure shit got done
i made sure we got to school early, which he hated
for free breakfasts

which came with the free lunch program
sometimes those were the only meals we had
so i didn't care if he got mad
we played "school"
long before he was even in school
meaning i made him do my homework
and while that made me
the short term winner
it made my younger Brother smart
smarter than me
reading from the dictionary
at age three.
seriously.
I'm not making that shit up.
ask him.

we used to play a game
i'm not sure if i made it up
or someone older taught it to me
called TRIP
where i would have my Brother going past me
back and forth
trying to get by
without getting tripped.
truth is you can pretty much trip the person every time
but you cat and mouse
and let them get by
so they think they are winning
then lift their legs out from under them
for a hard ass fall
i really thought that shit was funny

years later
my Mom pointed out how
in all the pictures of us
as little kids

that survived the evictions
- I mean the pictures
it is a miracle we have photos at all

"it's so sweet, Leggs.
how you always have your arm around little Marty.
look! every single picture,"
my Mom celebrated.

it wasn't EVERY picture.
and dang! she was right, it was most of 'em.

i hadn't noticed.
i'm so grateful she showed me that.

on another occasion
i was yucking it up
about how great it is to be an oldest child
and pick on yer little brother.
don't let anyone else beat him up
except me.
Ha Ha Ha.
i laughed.

a friend pointed out
from their youngest child perspective
how
ignorant
and not funny
that is

and i shut my trap.
i was
like

damn.

later
i brought this up
to Marty
and i could see
by his expression
that he wasn't ready
for this conversation and that
i had, in fact
caused
him
Harm

and i felt my heart drop in my chest
i couldn't joke my way out of this

as an older sibling
and a child
who protected and cared
i was also
mean and a bully
to my Brother.

i wish i could take that back.
but there's no take backs.
i sure am grateful
that my Brother Marty was born.
i wouldn't have survived without him.

call me if it gets bad

If I tried to sit down and name all the different places I lived, it would take Some Time. And I know I would not remember every place. I would need clues. I would hafta research, visit documents, old movies I made, call my younger brother Marty, ask the interweb.

I could free-write and recall different memories, then try to remember where I was living at the time of the memory. Cuz that's a trick, too. Maybe I was just crashing on someone's couch. "Staying over South," I'd say to my friends at the drop-in center. There were places I stayed at, or when I was hopping around, and had to use someone else's address, so I could still get mail, to access resources. To pretend I had "housing stability." I tried so hard as an adult to have and keep my own place, and did it a few times, and struggled. The longest address I ever stayed at my whole life was a supportive housing program.

I "inadvertently brought the chaos of childhood into my adult life," is one way I've talked about it. Maybe it's the T from PTSD, maybe it's a neurodivergent brain, maybe it's all the times I forgot things on purpose so I wouldn't get in trouble, that I have a hard time remembering my own address. Maybe it's fetal alcohol syndrome or the impact of my own chemical use, multiple concussions, or that I was dropped on my head as a kid. I'm not saying that shit to be funny, though I have at my own expense in the past. I've had too many addresses to count and I've also gone without.

While I can't recall my own address, I do remember my Gramma Ganser's. I was 36 when my Gramma Ganser joined the Ancestors, and I still know her phone number by heart. The phone number I've known my whole life. Brains are interesting. Memory that folks will call "selective." Her house was small, one level. Bunch of ramblers in a row, postage stamp yards with basements and a garage. Stacked close together almost like an unending ice cube tray, if you backed way out and looked down, like the clouds.

She lived on Juniper Street in so-called Coon Rapids, Minnesota. They say the city is named for raccoons, but people keep trying to change it so we don't have to say a racial slur when we say where we're from.

The streets were alphabetical, and named for trees.
Iris, Juniper, Kumquat, Larch.
Magnolia, Norway, Olive, Pine.

I loved the weeping willow in my Gramma Ganser's front yard that would hold me when I was little. Among her favorite flowers were morning glories, blue and opening up with the morning sun. They were annuals she would plant each year, like the short little orange and yellow marigolds, that I did not like the smell of back then. She always grew rhubarb in the back yard, in that same spot behind the garage. She would make rhubarb crumble baked in a big cake pan. She would take us to Zantigo for chilitos, before I got my first job there, back before they got bought out by Taco Bell.

My Gramma Ganser was a nurse, and the one I would call if I injured myself, or was sick, or for medical advice. Into adulthood, I even called her when I was scared. Sometimes late at night. Sometimes in undiagnosed manic episodes, sometimes drunk. I always called her when I was cooking something from scratch.

Damn I would love to tell my Gramma Ganser what I've learned about growing food, plants, and flowers, over the past eight years. It took me a minute to slow down as a grown up and connect with Momma Earth, long after my Gramma Ganser's death. It also took access to land for me to really put my hands in it. Putting in The Work in cross-class relationships brings so much healing, especially in intimate relationships. I want to tell her that. Intimacy only works when the other person and I get vulnerable and real and are all in. Stability of Home makes all that possible. There's lots of things you can only REALLY access with an address.

Let me just say it! "Hey Gramma, I am in a relationship with a person I love and they love me too and we put in hard work to be together, a cross-class intimate relationship, and it is so healing. I'm sober again and we live in a house together with two dogs, two cats and a lot of plants! I chalk hearts on the sidewalk with the names of Loved Ones lost to poLice terror, which I think you would understand now, as an Ancestor, since your husband, my Grandpa, who died before I was born, was a sheriff. Bringing love and healing is my Life's Work. I'm growing rhubarb that my friend Jude gifted me, which I never would have chosen, and it reminds me of you. This year I have grown a huge, untidy row of corn, and so many marigolds that I now love the smell of! When I am surprised to love the smell, I think of you. Nomy made me a garland of the big orange blooms and I hung it on a mirror that was my Mom's, near the front door of our home, like a big smile. I look in that mirror and I get hugged by all five of you, Nomy, Jude, my Mom, Momma Earth and You."

When my Gramma Ganser died, from Cancer and/or its aggressive treatments, with her went the amazing gatherings of my Father's side of the family. She was the glue that held the family together, our Matriarch.

Turkey, her savory stuffing, slow baked ham covered in pineapple and maple syrup, potatoes with cheese, lefse, sweet potatoes, mashed potatoes with gravy, these were the big holiday foods, and I mean she really did it up. I don't know how she pulled it off. I took those delicious meals for granted until I tried to do a similar thing myself for a bunch of people. Honestly, I couldn't do it, not the way she did. Her cooking was my favorite, and her house was super fun. There was always football on tv and soccer being played in the back yard, my Uncle Bill was especially good at soccer. If Bill and my Uncle Paul played, we would get a really good game with kids and adults going. We always let the little kids score goals.

My Gramma used to be one of the people I would call as kids when we were out of groceries. It would get rough when there was no food at home and the only meals Marty and I ate were at school. When weekends arrived with bare cupboards, that meant we had to get food. One of the times my Gramma Ganser came and brought us groceries, she asked me to come back and talk to her after she handed off the bags. We went inside and put away the stuff that needed to stay cold, and then I went back out to her car. I hoped I wasn't in trouble.

It was hot outside, we were living in the apartments near Fedor's Market. She had the AC on in her big, brown Thunderbird, and I got in. I hated having to ask her for food. I was worried about what she might say. She asked me how things were. I didn't tell her much. Then she looked me square in the blue eyes, and told me, with her thick Minnesota accent (that later she swore she never had - the movie Fargo offended her), "If it ever gets really bad, you can call me, and I'll come get you. I love you and little Marty so much."

I remember thinking both *how bad would it hafta get to be "really bad"?* and *I'm never gonna tell anyone how bad it is.* And what I quickly said was "thank you," and went inside to see the treasures she brought us and totally chow down.

walk down to k-mart to buy some shoes

my younger brother lost a shoe
i have no idea how
a kid could lose just one
shoes are usually together
like my brother and I were.

we gathered up loose change
coins in the couch cushions and chairs
checked every pocket of every clothes or jacket
a couple bucks from Mom and we headed to the mall

i made up a song, as i often did
to pass the time or make things fun
influenced by tv (our babysitter) and top 40 music
to the tune of Eddy Grant's Electric Avenue
a song I know now is about Black uprising
and the violence of poverty

we're gonna walk down to
k-mart to buy some shoes
and then we'll go to northtown

we sang that song silly
over and over
and all the way home

two and a half miles
is a long way for a kid
only wearing one shoe

jerry's leftovers

we lived with him a long time
he was a bass player
in a local mounds view rock band
i remember one of the bands he was in
was called sluggo
like the villain
from mr. bill on SNL

that's how my Mom met him
when his band was playing
at a bar - The Mermaid
he was popular, ran with a crew
guys from his bands
guys on motorcycles
the people who bought drugs from him

i think my Dad
dislocated his thumb
on my Mom's face
over it
jerry and my Mom hooking up, I mean
at The Mermaid

jerry had long, red hair
handlebar mustache
extremely tall
his favorite tv show was M*A*S*H
which i hated
he always got first pick of the tv shows
so i've seen every episode

there were things we always had when jerry was around
we always had bacardi
fixadent
2 liter bottles of coke
jerry didn't like ice cubes from a tray
so we mostly always had ice cubes
from the store
in the freezer
in a bag
so many things for grown ups and not for Us

almost always there was a massive pile of weed
and a big old school scale
back when there was stems and seeds
we didn't always have food
but jerry was the weed man

borrowing a cup of sugar
would advance to
borrowing a sandwich.
you gotta be really nice
and super
exhaustingly
performative
and
swallowing yer pride
to borrow food.
especially if you never made good on the loan.

jerry really liked american chinese food
chicken chow mein. pork fried rice.
chicken egg foo young. egg rolls.
he would come home with these huge brown bags
with the receipt stapled to them
smelled so fricken good.
in those cool white paper pails with the wire handles.
always extra rice.

sometimes
just sometimes
Marty and I would get the leftovers
if there were any.
usually not.

those sometimes when we got jerry's leftovers
it would often just be
the brown egg foo young gravy
and white rice
and that was sooooooo delicious.
adding water stretched it a little further.

Marty and i would be in our own ritual.
especially the first week or two of the month
because that meant food stamps brought us groceries
taking turns from meal to meal
cutting the frozen pizza in half,
then the other guy gets to pick which half they want.
if yer the cutter you work real hard making portions equal
If there were more kids around it meant
making more portions
we ate a lot of campbell's soup
and hamburger helper back then

toward the end of living with my Mom and jerry
around the time when they found a way to turn food stamps
into money into drugs and chinese food
when i was in 6th and 7th grade
they stopped looking for small apartments
to get kicked out of
and advanced to duplexes
to get kicked out of
bigger places with basements and garages
fancy neighborhoods
neighborhood kids with atari
and expensive off-road bicycles

bigger homes meant more roommates
lots of what nosey neighbors and kops would call "traffic"
the big place meant jerry's band could practice there
that sounds cool
and it really wasn't
we were the party house
dude practicing his keyboard part with a metronome
to supertramp's "bloody well right"
All
Night
Long

i don't really remember any conversations with jerry
when i think of him, i do see his smile.
he never tried anything
it sucks that i hafta say that about men
they kept late nights

when i was 30 i was in Amsterdam
for a film festival
using a passport for the first time
surrendering my "linear sobriety"
for free drinks on the plane, bacardi cokes
at a cafe, i watched my friend roll a crappy joint
how could i - someone who had never been high
be a judger of a joint like that
i had avoided weed, i was mad at it
after watching another sloppy joint be rolled
i, surprisingly, offered a service i did not know i had
and started rolling perfect joint after perfect joint
like a perfect joint making machine
rolling them so tight between fingers and thumbs
i was detaied and quick, even giving a twist to the ends
i rolled every drop of marijuana in sight
my friend was kinda shocked.
thanks, jerry.

my mom's voice

my Mom's voice had a rugged texture
damn i miss it.
she's one of the few people i would say was a Tough Broad
there aren't many people i would call a tough broad.
wait.
i would also call her Mom a tough broad
and her Mom's Mom a tough broad

i come from a line of Tough Broads

when i was a baby my Mom recorded her voice
reading books, she would play them at night.
those recordings put me right to sleep
for a number of years
Marty, too.
i can't hear them in my head when i try to remember,
but i can feel how held i felt just to listen
my Mom's young voice, talking so sweet
readin' little kid books
without actually being there
i really wish i still had those Mom books on tape.

we would watch The Muppet Show together
and my Mom would do all the voices.
she was good at 'em too!
"derpity derp mort ort," she would do The Swedish Chef
my Mom was so funny
she laughed at my jokes
she let us watch Saturday Night Live
from the very first season

it was especially fun if she was home watching it with us.

when i came out, my mom joined PFLAG
she told me and some of my friends a joke
"what do you call a lesbian dinosaur?" my Mom asked
i thought for a moment, cuz i should know
"lickalottapuss" she said, and busted out laughing
i got a lot of mileage out of that joke
and i always footnote her

my Mom's laugh
even her giggle
hearty and deep
Raspy

she had us buying her cigarettes from a young age
sending us with a note
up the street to the corner store
saratogas, Marty reminded me
not yet the marlboro 100s soft pack

later she was always "quitting smoking"
ordered by the doctor
at home on oxygen
chain smoking capris
which are quite possibly, the worlds skinniest cigarettes
the little box with the most pink on it.

"Leggs, on yer way here, could you pick up some smokes?"
she'd ask.

it was hard to say no.

damn, I miss her laugh

trying to be cool

i got it in my head that i should shave my legs
even though there was nothing much to see
other girls at school
were talking about it

my Mom was
in the living room
surrounded by people and music
and laughter and drinks
i had already put Marty to bed
my Mom had brought shaving up to me before
and i was a hard no
so i figured she'd be excited
cuz girl stuff

"hell yeah, Leggs!" my Mom said all playful and excited.
my Mom's nickname for me was Leggs
she said it was cuz my legs were so long
i liked it when she called me that
i was skinny and blonde and
probably needed a bath more than a shave
"go for it! use the pink shaver. you've watched me. might as
well shave yer arms too, while yer at it. you got this."

i feel like i flew
up a set of stairs
so we musta been living
in one of the duplexes then
with another family

i shaved.
it was satisfying.
lathering up with
thick bubbly bar of soap
then making long paths
like a hot wheels car
driving down a little dirt road
til both legs were shiny and clear

i was so proud of myself
i barely dried off
and wrestled
with my PJs
to get them back on
my Mom wanted to see
even though it was way past my bedtime
i stood tall as i walked down the stairs
toward the smell of weed and booze
to the crowd of people
all my fans
i smiled about as big as i felt
and i showed her

and she said

"you shaved your WHOLE arms? You were only sposta shave
yer arm PITS!!!"

Ha! Ha! Ha!
everyone laughed.

what a dummy.

storage wars

i was a grown up at 12
big orange school bus
little apartment buildings
tucked way back
behind the transmission center
smell of exhaust, air so dry
field of long dead grass
my younger brother and I
followed the little street
back to the dirty, stucco apartments
clowning, care free, little rugrats

uh oh, there's our landlord's car
and a moving truck
what the fuck? men in matching outfits
packing up our stuff
tearing down the posters
from our shared bedroom wall
time to move again
sad cuz I was just feeling settled
how did my Mom swing this hired help?

perfect strangers
"just doing their job"
throwing our belongings
with little consideration
into brown moving boxes
or into the trash
not very careful, but still
moving SO FAST

fancy! I thought!
professional movers!

"can we help?"
we asked the men in blue coveralls
after all, we were experienced at this routine
and we would use more care
"go find the landlord" they said
so we went in search of the landlord

"can we help?"
we asked the landlord who was sweaty and wearing a tie
he seemed bothered by us
and was talking shit about my Mom
we were just trying to help
"go find your Mother" he said

"can we help?"
we ask our Mom who is in our neighbor's unit
upstairs, upset, uprooted again
drunk and high and hyperfocused
"whoa they let you in?" my Mom asked.
"go back in there! get your homework, a change of clothes and
your favorite game, and get back up here right away. hurry!
GO!"

quite possibly
one of the most important things
she ever asked us to do
homework, change of clothes, favorite game
but we didn't know that
we coulda grabbed it all
i think we maybe grabbed our homework
just the clothes on our back, my tan britannias
i don't remember where we went that night
or if we even ate dinner
probably not

and we
Never
saw
any of that stuff
Ever again.

all of our belongings
everything our family owned
from the kitchen, the bathroom, the living room,
my Mom and jerry's room, our winter clothes in the closet,
all of it, furniture, beds, photographs, toys,
got thrown out or packed up and put into "storage."
i remember learning later that it was just $350
that was owed to get our stuff back
and my Dad didn't step in and pay it
i know my Mom asked him.
someone could have paid it, and rescued us
but i guess they were sick of bailing my Mom out.
so there we were, UNhoused again.
swept away like garbage. Displaced.
punished for being Poor.

At night, instead of sleep, I would think about all those things
we lost, and where they might have gone.

My kid brain imagined, a detailed scenario, a sort of annual
poLice and politrickster family party and auction, where
poLice are out of their costumes, and with their families. I
would see in my mind hundreds of white, happy, suburban
families and really shiny people, housed people, wearing
brand new clothes with fresh new haircuts gathered merrily
outside. And there's tents and canopies and a big bouncy
house. And it's festive, people are having sodas, and there's
lots of food around. Little kids are laughing and jumping
in potato sacks, like you see on tv. I see carnival rides and
clowns and people are getting their faces painted.
And then there's this auction. There's cars and boats and

impounded vehicles people couldn't afford to get back and other stuff that the poLice stole from people that is now "for sale." Off to the side of the auction there's all these brown boxes, people are bartering for them.

I lean into this vision I've created and squint my kid eyes, and I recognize these boxes! They are from our Home! One of the boxes says "KIDS ROOM" with a black magic marker. I can still smell it, like the movers just wrote the words in our bedroom. I picture this spoiled, resourced, snotty, little bully of a kid eating a fucking snow cone, who turns to his parents and says, "Daddy, Daddy, I want this one. Daddy, I want the one that says Kid's Room."

A little auction session happens and the box goes to the kop family for 50 cents. The kid tosses his snowcone aside and rips into the box, not giving a shit about most of it.

I'm helplessly watching all mine and Marty's belongings, in slow motion, being mostly discarded. Oh my God, there's that soccer ball that I got for Christmas last year. I hadn't even opened it yet, I hadn't taken it out of the box. I forgot about that! And there's my certificate for participating in basketball, my huge stuffed teddy bear Grover, who was falling apart and re-sown together by my Mom - I'm so sorry Grover!

And the little kid who doesn't need any of this shit, this kid grabs one thing, some arbitrary item, holds it up like a trophy, and then just leaves everything else on the ground. His sister comes and looks, she doesn't want any of that Kid's Room crap. They just sweep everything else away.

survivor love letter

february 14, 2020

Little Lisa,
i love you little lisa
i love you little lisa
i love you big lisa
YOU DESERVE TO BE LOVED & NURTURED
the flowers grow especially for you!

Tear Drops
are Flower Petals
are Words

share your experience
keep growing

it's okay to remember
it's okay to forget
IT WAS NOT YOUR FAULT
tend to yourself
tend to the land

Love yourself very very Much
then even MORE
Love, Lisa

#SurvivorLoveLetter #metoo
www.survivorloveletter.com
thanks to Tani Ikeda

[image: drawing and collage of me as a little blonde-haired, white, 3 year old survivor kid with unbrushed hair and big eyes. there are tear drops/flower petals of cut out flowers around my face and near my mouth. there are hearts all around me with the love letter hand written.]

thank you auntie kare kare

My Dad had his own place at some point, in a big apartment complex just on the other side of so-called Minneapolis, I say so-called now because it truly is Anishinaabe Territory. I think it was close to the city because I have a memory of riding in a car at night, mesmerized by the repetition of the freeway street lights overhead, and feeling happy. My Dad knew all the buildings' names in the skyline, the Foshay Tower was one he would talk about. He was so excited to take us up into the IDS tower, which at the time was the tallest building in the Twin Cities skylines. He always pointed out the IDS Tower.

Later in life my Dad told me a story. He was coming back into town from being on the road and was comforted to be welcomed back by his beloved Minneapolis skyline.

"Then, oh my god Lisa, I see there in the distance, one of the buildings was on fire!" my Dad told me. "I almost crashed looking to see which building it was, but I couldn't tell! I made it to your Gramma's and started making some calls, letting everybody know that there was a building in flames in downtown Minneapolis! I was shocked nobody had heard what was going on."

Came to find out, there wasn't a burning building at all. It was a new, big, obnoxious skyscraper, the Norwest building, which later became the Wells Fargo building, which is all lit up bright with yellow lights, and definitely not on fire. I thought it was so funny that my Dad panicked and mistook a new building for one burning up, and that he had made such a big deal about it. I also liked that my Dad was wrong. I used to joke with him late into adulthood, teasing him, the way he would give other folks a hard time. "Whoa, Dad, what's that big yellow building on fire?" He'd shoot me a look. Both my Dad and I liked giving people shit, making people laugh. Joke tellers, story tellers.

We got to my Dad's apartment, the building was fancy and big, and other family members were there. My cousin Kim, my Aunt Karen, other cousins and uncles. I think my Dad had a roommate at the time, and maybe this occasion was someone's birthday. The apartment complex had lots of young people living there, and my Dad seemed to be friendly with all of them. There was a workout room, outdoor patios where you could have a BBQ, and an indoor swimming pool! Even though it was nice outside, the pool seemed awesome, so my cousin Kim and I went in. My Aunt Karen made sure there was always someone older with us, after all, I couldn't swim.

I was walking back and forth across the pool, getting further and further toward the deep end. I was kinda bounce walking, teasing down the hill beneath me, as I got further and further away from safely being able to keep my head above water. My toes now just barely touching the bottom, criss crossing back and forth across the pool's width, bouncing me back up to breathe.

At some point, I slipped a little too far and when I put my toe down, all I hit was water, and I panicked. What was once me up high taking a deep breath, now filled my lungs with water. The bobbing up and down continued as I tried desperately to get myself up above water to breathe. With each effort, I sucked only water. I saw these two older kids on the edge of the pool, their legs dangling. I was like "HELP!" But I made no sound. I was screaming, doggie paddling with all my might, only to use every bit of energy I had. I saw my uncle Mike, he didn't stop what he had been doing the whole time, diving from the diving board over and over. I was trying so hard to save myself, and completely failing.

My life started flashing before my eyes. I saw my Mom holding me shortly after being born. I saw her accidentally grabbing a metal spoon instead of a wooden spoon, and spanking my bare toddler ass with it, then being so regretful afterwards about my bruised ass. I saw memory after memory that I would not know today had it not been for this near-death experience.

I wasn't done yet, what the hell!

I then felt calm come over me, as I gave up. I let death take me.

My Auntie Kare Kare told me when she came in, Mike was still diving, and I was lifeless at the bottom of the pool. She dove in and pulled me out, unconscious, and started pounding on my back and doing everything she could to revive me.

Suddenly, pulled from afterlife's comforting arms, I hacked up chlorine water and breathed a deep, painful, life-giving breath.

My Aunt Karen picked me up and carried me two flights back to my Dad's apartment. My arms were around her neck, she was holding me like a baby. I looked up at my Dad's only sister, a woman who would later help raise me, and I said, "Thank you, Auntie Kare Kare."

That night in the apartment I got anything I wanted, and I remember eating powdered donuts. My throat was raw and pained. Later in life, and still true today, I am unable to eat powdered donuts without my whole body reacting.

tan britannias

a snotty girl at school
was making fun of me
pointing out that my clothes were dirty

"are you Poor?" ha ha ha she laughed
"you wear those same pants everyday!
i haven't seen you wear anything else!
gross pig!"

i looked around
not wanting to lose
the new friends I had
who thought I was funny
new kid in school

"i love these tan britannias,
they are my favorite jeans,
i have three pairs," i lied.

"yeah, right.
let's see if the same stains are there tomorrow."

i loved my mom like this

when there wasn't a basketball team for girls my age
and i wanted to play, my Mom was not having it
i mean, like in a You don't get to tell me
what my Daughter does or does not do
kind of way.

outside activities for 2nd grade me
did get me outta her hair
and a couple of my friends
with parents who drove
were on the team

"of course my daughter is tough enough to play with boys
her age, she's been doing that her whole life," my Mom said.
"i already checked, there are no girls teams, yes i will come
down there, yes i will sign a waiver," she said.

my Mom went and got me on the boys team
my hero! That was so fun.
playing basketball three nights a week!
the parents always went to mcdonalds or DQ after too
my two favorite four-letter F words: free and food

in the second season i did get knocked in the face
with elbows quite a bit, the other team
always going for "the girl"
knocking me on my ass, trying to "teach me a lesson"
that i was in the wrong place
that this was the boys' club
their coach smiled

shit rolls downhill.

my last game was when i got knocked out cold on the floor
with a bloody nose and a concussion.

my Mom wasn't at the game, she never came to games, so
they had to call and track her down.

my Mom held me
so close
in the big front seat
of someone's car
on the way home
from the hospital
street lights
though the windshield
lighting up her face
with different colors
my Mom so concerned
she looked like an angel
telling me she loved me
speaking in her soft voice
my face against her
soft
suede
jacket
it was like no one else existed, just me and her
"i love you Leggs," she said.
i loved my Mom like this

and then from outta nowhere, i puked
all over my Mom's fancy new suede jacket
which broke my heart

"we can never have anything nice," Mom said.

i can tell

you can tell the people that have never
scrubbed public toilets for an hourly wage

i can tell the people who have never
went hungry, missed a meal
cuz poverty

when we were kids
extension cords and a nice neighbor
and keeping a good rapport
were the things that could save us
when the electricity got cut off

i'm glad that there are lots of people who have never had to
miss meals because there wasn't any. not even once. people
who were never malnourished because there wasn't enough.
i'm glad there are people who always had access to food, like
life long, you never even had to think about not having that
resource, especially not as a kid. food was provided, a given,
always there. like breathing.

i'm glad there are people who have always been housed.
some of you lived in the same house the whole time you grew
up. your whole life. never been evicted. never had someone
not renew your lease. never didn't know where you'd stay that
night, because there was no place to go, because you couldn't
afford it. always had housing stability, never even had to think
about it. i'm glad that there are people like that.

and sometimes you all are very frustrating.

like frustrating as fuck.

a pantry, tv trays and a pillowcase full of loot

a weekend road trip took us to Wisconsin
which gave my Mom a break from Marty and i
off to visit some of the Johnsons
my Gramma Ganser's side of the family, my Dad's Mom
maybe i was eight or nine years young
little blonde haired blue eyed rugrat
ripping down the highway in my Auntie Kare Kare's
little orange slug bug
Karen was always good for taking us on adventures
a working class super hero
rescuing us, even for one minute
the back seat felt like its own little fortress
laughing so hard i had snot bubbles coming outta my nose
with Karen's only child, my cousin Kim
Kim was even blonder than me,
strawberry blonde and freckle faced
in many ways Kim and i were like siblings, just one year apart
I stayed with them off and on as a kid.
and when we reunited, we wasted no time in having fun.

night was falling and there was snow outside
we settled into what felt like
the hugest house, and still humble
a place where the same people had lived for a very long time
the biggest room was overflowing with people,
lots of 2nd and 3rd cousins
happy kids and content grown ups
chatting it up, horsing around
sprawled out on couches and big comfy chairs
floor adorned with rugs and sleeping bags and pillows

38

blankets everywhere, there was not one uncomfortable spot
tv so big, you could see it from anywhere
even the fire was relaxed
with its crackling and popping
and the seemingly
unending
care
free
adding of logs
letting anyone who wanted to
take a turn
at tending the fire.
i could see that putting those logs on
was important to Marty.
he relaxed as he stared into the fire.
i felt proud of him, like i was his parent
everyone was being so nice

it was one of those homes where
there was a closet full of food
in addition to the cupboards
i always forget the name...
oh yeah, a "pantry"
they also had a free standing box freezer
like a massive white treasure chest
in addition to a fridge FULL of food
someone craved pizza rolls
POOF - pizza rolls
it felt like
if you wanted a certain snack
THEY HAD IT
sodas, cheetos, beef jerkies, oreos

"here Lisa, need a tv tray?" my Aunt Lynette asked.
the folding tray became my own personal table top feast.
Lynette is Karen's cousin like Kim and i are cousins.
"you need anything, you help yourself!"

i imagined myself making off like a thief
into the night
filling up pillow cases
like we did getting candy on Halloween.
my Mom really likes heath bars and red pistachios
they had both.

when you take away the pillow,
you can really pack a pillow case
full of loot.

a frozen pizza is a family meal.

i like not remembering if i did take any food home
without it being offered (but she did offer)
and i'm pretty sure i probably did.

there was a lot of hot cocoa and little bit of booze drinking
but no one got wasted and i didn't see anyone using drugs.
not even in a sneaky way thinking kids don't know what's up. i
didn't even smell pot the whole weekend.

when i think back, i picture myself
that weekend
like the fire
wild and kinda always moving and on guard.
also tended to
housed
relaxed

i remember wondering

wow

what would it be like to live like this, every day?

still housed haikus

always the phone first
if we had a phone at all
then the electric

we could see our breath
cuddled up on kitchen floor
oven door open

got school tomorrow
soon we will be evicted
trying to stay warm

no need for 911

we were visiting larry and sherri in so-called washington state
they were a couple, our mom & dad's close friends
i think one or both of them were god parents of marty or i,
i can't remember which
our dad wasn't with us, i think this is not long after he left
my mom was getting support
or maybe a little break
from trying to figure out
what the hell we were gonna do next

marty and i were at a park,
escaping ourselves
to the outdoors.
in this rich neighborhood
playing with a bunch of kids
brand new kids, wearing brand new clothes
we weren't quite fitting in and we were having fun

there was this older white dude that came up
he looked tired and the sun was hot
he found some shade under a tree
and plopped down for a nap.

kids were pointing and whispering about him
and checking him out from every angle
the sleeping man had shorts on, and some kids pointed out,
that if you bent down just right, you could see up this guy's
shorts, and see his balls.
funny.

witnessing passed out grown ups was familiar to me,
but here, out in the open
it was a different story

i was watching these kids surrounding
and teasing this guy
who I hoped was sleeping, and not dead

some kid called this sleeping man a "pervert"
then everyone else joined in
it wasn't long before some nosey ladies came around
i think some of them were parents of the kids
and then the kops showed up!

i was relieved that he woke up
the kops were rough with him
and then they took him away in handcuffs

i remember this event being such a big deal,
which didn't make sense
grown ups drilling kids for answers,
trying to get dirt on this guy, but he was clean
he didn't do anything, except sleep
and accidentally have his balls showing
and now he was off to jail,
i didn't know enough at that age to interrupt it or ask why

i was learning the word pervert,
and knowing that this guy was not it.
i was thinking about actual pervert guys i knew
who did fucked up things
who nothing would ever happen to
i was thinking about how if someone has a booger,
or their ass crack is showing, you could tell 'em
or you can invite an audience and charge admission

this guy didn't do anything except sleep outside

bad babysitters

I used to talk to my Mom about this one particular babysitter that I would see in my head. I really liked him. He looked like KC from KC and the Sunshine Band, only younger, and cuter.

That's the way, uh huh uh huh, I like it, uh huh uh huh...

He wore sporty solid color shorts with the white piping. A heartthrob kind of boy, straight outta the pages of Tiger Beat. A teenager who showed interest in me, always had a basketball with him. I liked him so much, and something was very wrong.

My Mom and Dad were young when I was born, 17 and 21. They were cool back then, they partied, they were parents and also made time to have fun. By the time I was their age, I was drinking with my mom, asking what was the deal with that guy with the basketball.

"Do you remember this babysitter, from when we lived in the yellow and white trailer, before Dad left?" I asked.

My Mom, Sam, got a look of dread and shut down. So I changed the subject. We were drinkin' buddies, so I would have chances to bring it up again.

I had this foggy memory, I was 5 or 6 years old, it was dark outside. I was on the couch, and my parents were upset and shaking me to wake up. I was naked and confused. So weird. Why wasn't I in bed? Why was I naked and out on the couch? How did I get there? Where was my little brother Marty?

I felt like I was in trouble, like I did something wrong. They had to work hard to keep me awake. I was groggy and uneasy on my feet. "Get to bed," my Mom told Little Lisa. But I needed help to do that, I had the top bunk.

"Who was that guy?" I asked my Mom, as I poured another bacardi coke. She started donkey crying.

"I'm so sorry Leggs, we didn't have another babysitter," she said. "We couldn't find anyone else. He was all we had."

I was like, damn. I put that one in the crock pot of my body mind for quite some time. It's still simmering on low. Cuz to me, that sounds a lot like that guy kept watching us, even after finding me passed out, drugged and naked on the couch.

A couple years later, and I'm back drinking with my Mom, she's in her own apartment now, upstairs. In the same building as my Grandma Cossolotto, her Mom. My Great Grandma Alta also had her own little unit in that brick building across the street from the high school. It was just me and my Mom, in her kitchen, none of her other friends were there.

"So, Mom. There have been a couple times when you or I have brought up that bad babysitter. If we're gonna bring this up, and it keeps happening while we're drinking, I want us to be able to, if we're going to talk about that, can we both AGREE to talk about it? Like, let's make sure we are both in an okay place to go there," I was saying.

We should hafta both consent, is what I was trying to negotiate, but I wasn't yet armed with that word. My Mom and I had never negotiated a boundary in our life. This was new and vulnerable territory. I got up while I talked, doing our beer rotation ritual, taking an ice cold beer from the freezer to drink, pulling another up from the fridge to replace it. My Mom fell a beer behind, and was lighting a cigarette.

I was saying, "let's agree beforehand, if we're going to talk about this, and if one of us says NO, then we drop it, because I feel like talking about this bad babystitter is bringing up some shit, that it's painful. And right now yer the one bringing it up. And I don't want to, I don't want to talk about it right now, I just can't, is that okay? What do you think?" I asked.

This felt like a risky request, I didn't want her to ask me to leave. Drinkin' together is how my Mom and I were connecting. And at the time, I loved what we had.

"If we don't both agree then let's not talk about it, okay?' I asked.

Something suddenly clicked in my Mom. She looked off in the distance and I would say she detached herself, left her body, and started talking without pause. My Mom was describing these horrific detailed things. Horrible things that happened over and over to this little girl, by a number of men. This was not the memory I had been talking about.

And at the time, I was like, *I don't remember this shit happening to me. Why is my Mom making this up? What the fuck.* I was young and assumed it was about me. I felt like that confused, naked, little kid in the trailer.

I realized later, my Mom was describing in detail, some traumatic shit that had happened to her.

There was a summer that Marty and I went away to Michigan to spend time with my Mom's older sister and her family. While we were out there, we stayed at one of our grandpa's place for awhile. He was actually my Mom's step dad. My Mom was livid when she learned we were there. We were sposta be at our Aunts, not the step grandpa's. I had only just learned we had another grandpa when we got there.

He brought us to the flea market and bought me a pair of tan britannias. He had a huge wood shop and let us build things and play with the tools. It was such a cool place. We had so much access to stuff we'd never even seen before. SO FUN.

Later my Mom kept grilling me about what that guy did, did he touch me? Protective Momma Bear, grilling me about the wrong guys.

"Did he do anything to you, did he touch you?" she was so upset.

was this the guy
from the story?
had he invited
other men in?
this man
who didn't hurt me
had done
terrible things
to my Mom
when she was a kid.

tomboy

substitute teacher called me "señor"
instead of "señorita"
everyone laughed

someone says
"this is the girls bathroom"
as if I don't know that

mad because marty got a football
and I got a crappy doll

crying on my mom's shoulder again

"what's wrong with me?" I asked.

"there's nothing wrong with you, Leggs. yer a Tomboy," my
Mom said.

WHAT!!!???

my body relaxed inside itself
you mean there's something else!?!?!

clouds began to part
for about twelve seconds
until I realized that
being a tom-boy
still meant that I was a girl.

weekends with dad

My Dad's job while I was growing up, was as a traveling salesman - selling the advertisements on bowling score sheets. I thought that was cool. This was back before electronic scoring, back when everything was on paper. Providing something people needed, if they were gonna bowl. This work took him out of town a lot, across the US, which was a bummer for me, probably fun for him.

My Dad would often bring us with him to the local bowling alleys he was working and kinda set us free. He would set us up for unlimited bowling and hand us a roll of quarters to play all the pinball and video games we wanted. And if the bowling alley had food (they usually had a bar), we would sometimes get french fries, deep fried mushrooms, burgers or pizza, while he worked. He sometimes took me with him when he would drive around looking for businesses to cold call, creating lead lists, on those yellow lined "legal pads," sometimes letting me be the one taking notes. I learned writing in all caps from my Dad, I liked that. I heard his cold calling, sales pitches and follow ups. I learned how to sell - and later used those skills to found and direct a film festival. Now I've adapted those skills to do Radical Redistribution of resources. You can really take almost any skill, and use it for collective liberation.

My Dad taught me a lot of things. He taught me to bowl, like the proper form, and he stressed it was important to break a hundred each game. I learned flirting from my Dad, he was handsome, a sweet talker and a flirt. He taught me how to drive, in his car that had a fuzz buster, and I was a lead foot outta the gate. My Dad (with assistance from my Uncle Paul) taught me that if you are a teenager and get a car stuck in a snow bank, and don't tell yer Dad, you will get caught later when the car is inside a garage, and the snow melts, cuz big puddle. My Dad showed me that if you had a JC Penney's card, you could use that to get school clothes, or your first bra. I learned to like neighborhood barber shops from my Dad.

I know he taught me how to ride a bike, even tho I don't remember that, cuz my Mom told me. I also don't remember him teaching me to tie my shoes, but I know he did that too, cuz i do it a weird, messed up, left handed way, and I'm right handed.

I learned the not good enoughs from my Dad. Nothing I did was good enough. I learned from my Dad that doing work that didn't make money wouldn't win his approval. He wasn't impressed when my movies played in Brazil or premiered at the Walker Art Center, but he'd brag that I worked on a Norelco commercial that played during a superbowl. My Dad called me a lesbian, like it was a bad word, before I was even out. It only happened a few times when he was drunk, but it was enough to make an impact.

My Dad taught me how to pop the world's greatest popcorn in the kettle. I'm so skilled at popping almost every kernel and not burning it, as long as I'm familiar with the stove I'm using. And it's all my Dad. He would pop popcorn with the perfect blend of butter and salt, filling brown paper bags with it, and we'd bring 'em all half greasy to the drive-ins. My Dad was all about the drive-ins. Cooler full of generic pop, he loved root beer, so I did too. He'd bring us early so we could swing on the swingsets and stay late past the scary movie. I love the drive-ins. I am a lot like my Dad. Someone who works with what they got. He would put a can of corn and hot dogs into hamburger helper, and call it a "Ganser Special."

My Dad came to so many of my sports and art and music things, into adulthood. While he was absent a lot of my childhood, he definitely showed up in ways that my Mom, who was my anchor, could not. Although, my Mom would remind me of the times I would sit up all night at the window, waiting for him to come get us, and not get my precious weekend.

One weekend we spent with our Dad, he was staying in my Gramma Ganser's unfinished basement, and he had this awesome stereo set up. It was the first thing I saw when we got there. Marty and I were so excited, we barely put our stuff down and my Dad was letting us put the records on ourselves, softly laying the needle on the vinyl. We listened, sang and danced to my Dad's record collection for hours. Lots of top 40 and Pop music, with the warm, rich sound of vinyl, such a tactile ritual and fond analog memory. The album covers had liner notes with the lyrics. Marty and I were into learning lyrics and we were singing along to Stevie Wonder, The Beatles, Elton John, Queen, Barry Manilow... It's ironic that most of these records were gay guys. The first record I ever owned was Elton John's Greatest Hits. I loved every song on that album, and sung every syllable. My Dad bought me that. With one of those little, white, portable plastic kid record players. Both of which we didn't keep for long. My Mom would return things we got as gifts for money, so we could buy food.

I never knew me a better time, and I guess I never will

My Dad popped us the big question, like grown ups do, "What do you kids wanna be when you grow up?"

"I wanna be a lawyer or a singer," I said. "A lawyer because they're rich." If one of us was rich, we could take care of everybody, good thinkin'.

My Dad said, "Lawyers hafta go to school for a really long time."

51

"Oh," I said, disappointed, cuz school was expensive. "Well I can't be a singer, cuz there's no girl singers," I said.

"What?!?" exclaimed my Dad, "There's lots of girl singers! What do you mean?" My Dad was shocked.

"I mean look here," I said as I thumbed through my Dad's albums. "There's no girl singers here, no lead singers anyway, not even musicians anywhere on any of these records. The girls are the fans," I said.

"There's lots of women singers, Lisa," my Dad said.

"Yeah right," I muttered.

It wasn't long and my Dad took off to run an errand and came back with a huge stack of new albums from the record store, all women! He played Diana Ross, Olivia Newton John, Janis Joplin, Donna Summer, Captain & Tennille, Carole King...

My young Dad curated me and Marty an early eighties Ladyfest. We danced and sang the night away. He showed a little non binary girl me, that YES there were LOTS of Women lead singers, and that I could be one, if I wanted to.

Rest in Power Martin "Marty" Ganser Jr. Born September 20, 1947, died from COVID-19 on January 25, 2021

alone together

i made it to the seventh grade
into a junior high
where I had attended
4 out of the 5
elementary schools
that funneled kids there

the first day of school came and went
with ease
i was established
instead of new
and, dare i say, popular?!?

i practically danced home
past our neighbors' huge houses
tidy flower beds in early autumn bloom
fresh cut lawns
literal picket fence
to find my Mom
defeated on the couch

"i'm sorry, Leggs. i tried. we gotta be outta here by 8am
tomorrow. i don't know where we're gonna go. we are out of
places to go," my exhausted Momma sobbed.

i stood there a moment
my school books still in my hands
the clock was ticking
such a rare occasion

my Mom
and i
alone
together

"i'm done," i said to my Mom as i scooped the coins from the
table she was slumped over. "i'm gonna go get Marty from the
bus stop," i said.

i gathered up what little we had
into a pillowcase
homework, toothbrushes, soccer stuff
and walked away

"what are we gonna do?' Marty asked.

"call Gramma Ganser," i said confidently.

people just kept passing by
driving home from work
the cars and trucks seemed
fresh off the lot
as we walked
to the nearest pay phone
my mind was racing
i heard the familiar growl
of my Brother's stomach.

"how was school?" i asked.

i was making decisions for both of us
that would impact us for the rest of our lives.

escape to the blueberries

For a while, as a grown up, I would run errands for my Mom. I'd help her keep her clean her bird cage, take out her garbage, make sure she had what she needed. I even brought her pot a few times, I could see what she was getting wasn't right. I would grocery shop for her. It always took so long cuz her lists were all over the place, and she'd send me into Cub, this big grocery store over by Northtown Mall. Sometimes I would pitch in a few bucks, get her things that weren't on the list. Special treats. I was trying to get her to eat less processed food, and also not take away the choices she was making. She had a hard time keeping weight on, disabled and chronically ill. She got foods that were easy to make. There were organic blueberries on sale and they tasted delicious, so I got her a pint.

When I got back to my Mom's apartment I had to rush off after putting away her groceries, instead of sticking around like I usually would. Later, I saw that she sent a couple texts and also tried to call. "Leggs, I need to talk to you about the blueberries," she said. I was thinking, *uh oh*. Maybe she didn't know what to do with them, or was upset because they're expensive. I texted that I paid for them and that I was sorry for getting things not on the list. She said she couldn't text about it, she had to talk to me. So I called her. She told me a story, the way she once in awhile would. A vibrant, colorful story of her childhood that was not about trauma. It was the balm for the trauma. Eating those blueberries straight from the package brought my Mom back to the last time she remembered eating blueberries. Tears welled up in my eyes and the hair raised on my arms. I've always said that my

Mom was an unrealized poet, and you know what? Maybe my favorite poet, without ever having written one poem. I wrote this poem from my Mom's story.

please run free, little girl
knock-kneed, summer breeze
michigan by the water
face and hands
stained purple blue
tummy so full
almost sick you said!
running, laughing
escaped
to the blueberries
you are healed
you are the sword you wield
you were meant to be
exactly how you are right now
to be free.

I wrote the following lyrics on the plane, ten days after Nomy's Mom, Malinda died. Nomy and I were on our way to so-called Coon Rapids to pull my Mom off life support. Ten days between two Matriarchal deaths.

Sometimes the tools
We use, We choose
To survive
Take Our Lives

and I thought
that You and I
would have more Time.

Rest in Power Mom, Sandra "Sam" Ganser, born September 20, 1951, left to join the Ancestors on October 7, 2017

acknowledgements

First I say miigwech, thank you, to the Original People and Native ancestors of the land I grew up on, the Dakota, Lakota People, the Anishinaabe, in so-called Minnesota. Thank you to everyone who kept me alive and who helped me write this book. Thank you to my Ancestors. Thank you to Momma Earth and thank you to my Mother, Sam Ganser, for squeezing me out and holding me. The two of you are now one, and I will keep tending. Thank you to my Father, Marty Ganser, whose favorite color was green, I am surrounded by you. Thank you to Pauline Ganser, Bernice Cossolotto, Karen Ganser and Alta Balderston. Thank you Little One, Scruffy, Tigger, Kingston and Pearl Buttons.

Thank you to the Matriarchs, young and old, and those just emerging. Thank you to Kimi Jo Frey and Megan Ganser. Thank you to my community and family, chosen and blood. Thank you to all the grown ups outside my family system who nurtured and fed me. Thank you to the anti poLice-terror community, to all survivors of poLice violence and folks who lost Loved Ones to poLice murder. Thank you to all the Femmes, Fatties, Black, Indigenous and People of Color, Disabled, Sex Workers, Trans Women, Harm Reduction workers, Abolitionists, friends who survived the Prison Industrial Complex, all of you radical thinkers with different life experience than me - I learn so much from you. Thank you to my Trans and Queer Elders. Thank you La Mesha Irizarry and your Ancestor son Idriss Stelley, you told me I am one of your favorite writers before I was even published. Thank you to Jude Manley, Patricia Green, Friends of Bill & Bob, everyone at Gull Harbor & Squaxin Island Spiritual Fellowship. Thank you Talauna Reed for our Poverty Scholarship Book Club. Thanks to Terry Seracino and Sheelah Clarke, to Sheila Chad and yer Mom, to Earth Feather Sovereign and yer kids. Thanks to everyone who ever stood in as my "emergency contact person" or housed me without condition.

Thanks Dandelion dog, the animal family members including the Ganser-Lamm worms that help make the compost. Thank you Crystal Renee, and yer Ancestor Mama, Inez, I look forward to reading your books, BF. Thank you to my Brother, Marty Ganser, this book serves as a point of our connection and healing, which is forever.

Thank you to all the Poor and Indigenous folks with Poor Press and POOR Magazine. Thanks to everyone who has published with Poor: Tiny Gray-Garcia, Leroy F. Moore Jr, Muteado Silencio, Joey Villareal, Aunti Frances Moore, Audrey Candycorn, Dee Allen... for going first and speaking Truth. Thanks to my fellow Poverty Scholars in this 2021 writing cohort. Thank you Tiny Gray Garcia and yer Ancestor Mama Dee, you pulled me outta the procrastiNATION (as you say) and onto this heart opening path. Thank you to the teachings of POOR Magazine's PeopleSkool, which are woven into the fabric that holds my Life's Work. Thank you to my writing partner and zoommate, the Death Lady, Pearl Ubungen. Thanks to everyone who publishes with Poor in the future.

Thank you folks with class privilege who supported these books being published. Cross class relationships and radical redistribution of resources are healing balm. Thanks to Maya Ram (POOR Solidarity Fam facilitator) and Shani Banai (Access Support). Thanks most of all to my partner in life and love, from the top of this page to the bottom of my tender resilient heart, I love you Nomy Lamm. Thank you to yer Ancestor Mom, my friend, Malinda, and all your Ancestors and family for bringing you to where you are right now, interdependent with me.

i thought you might
break my heart
but you came to
break my fall

It was ((you)) who said "you should write that story down." A list of stories, the ones I tell a lot. I wasn't so sure, and I trusted you. You were right. Thank you.

Made in the USA
Las Vegas, NV
08 February 2022

43474562R00036